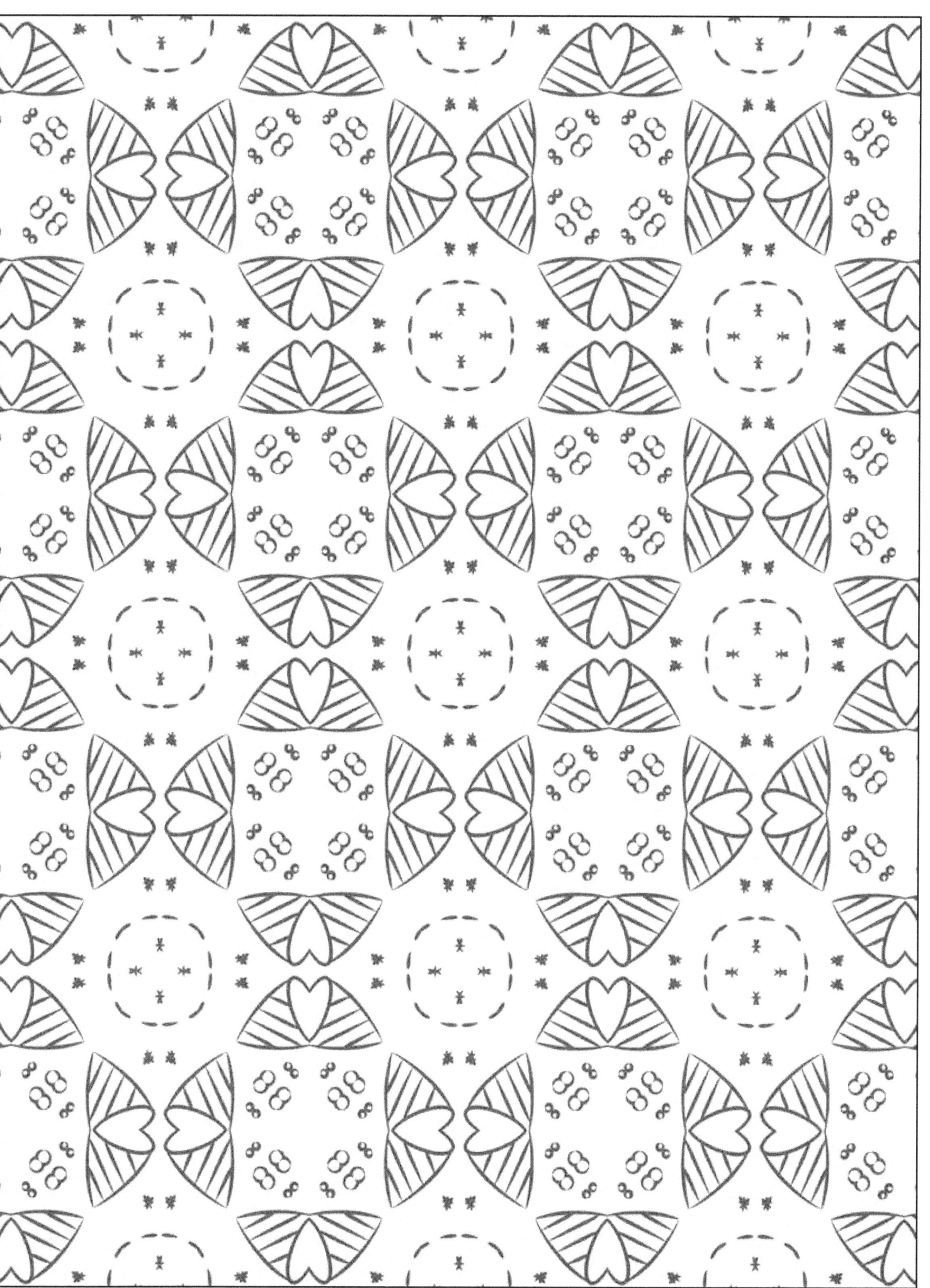

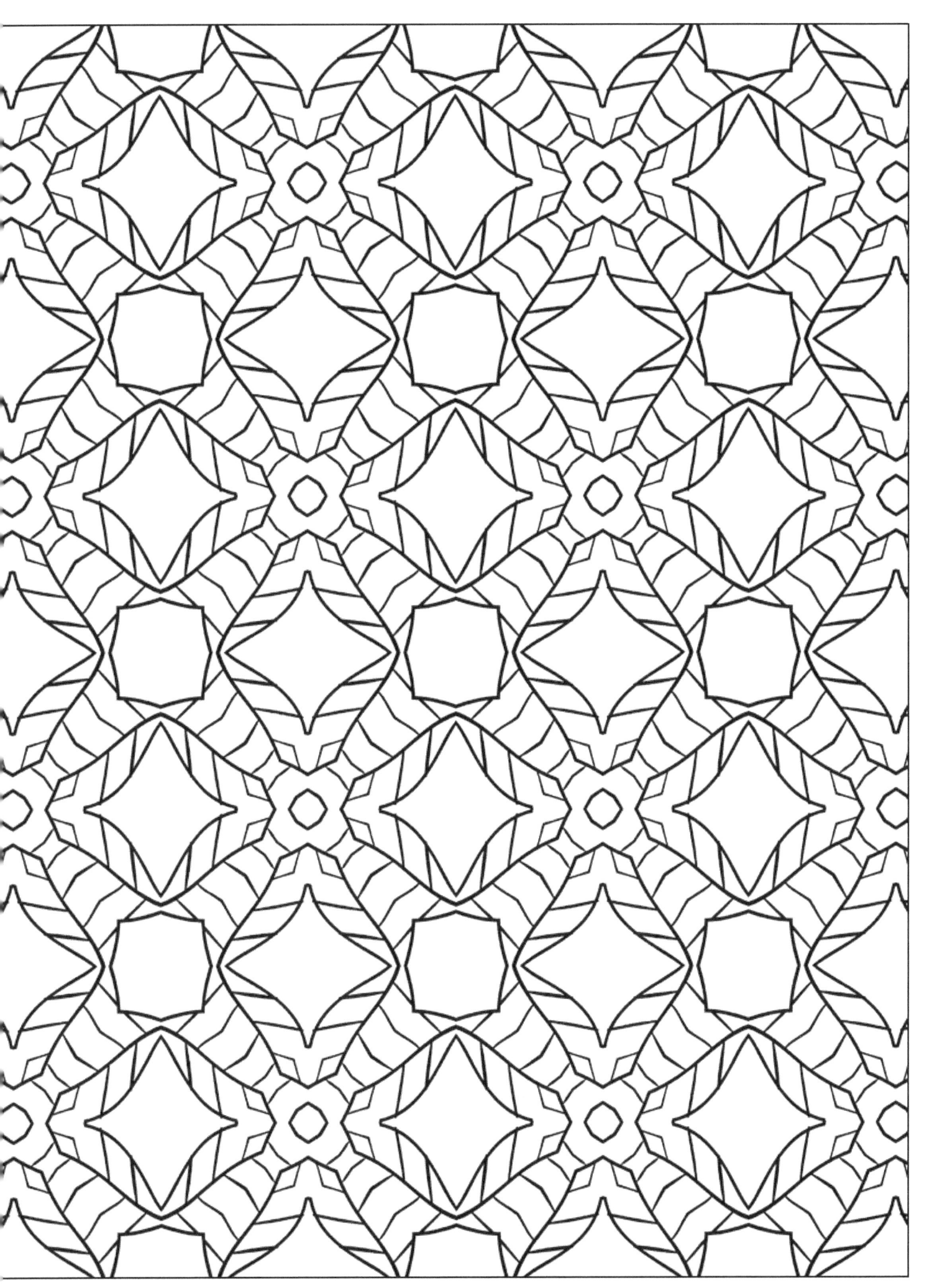

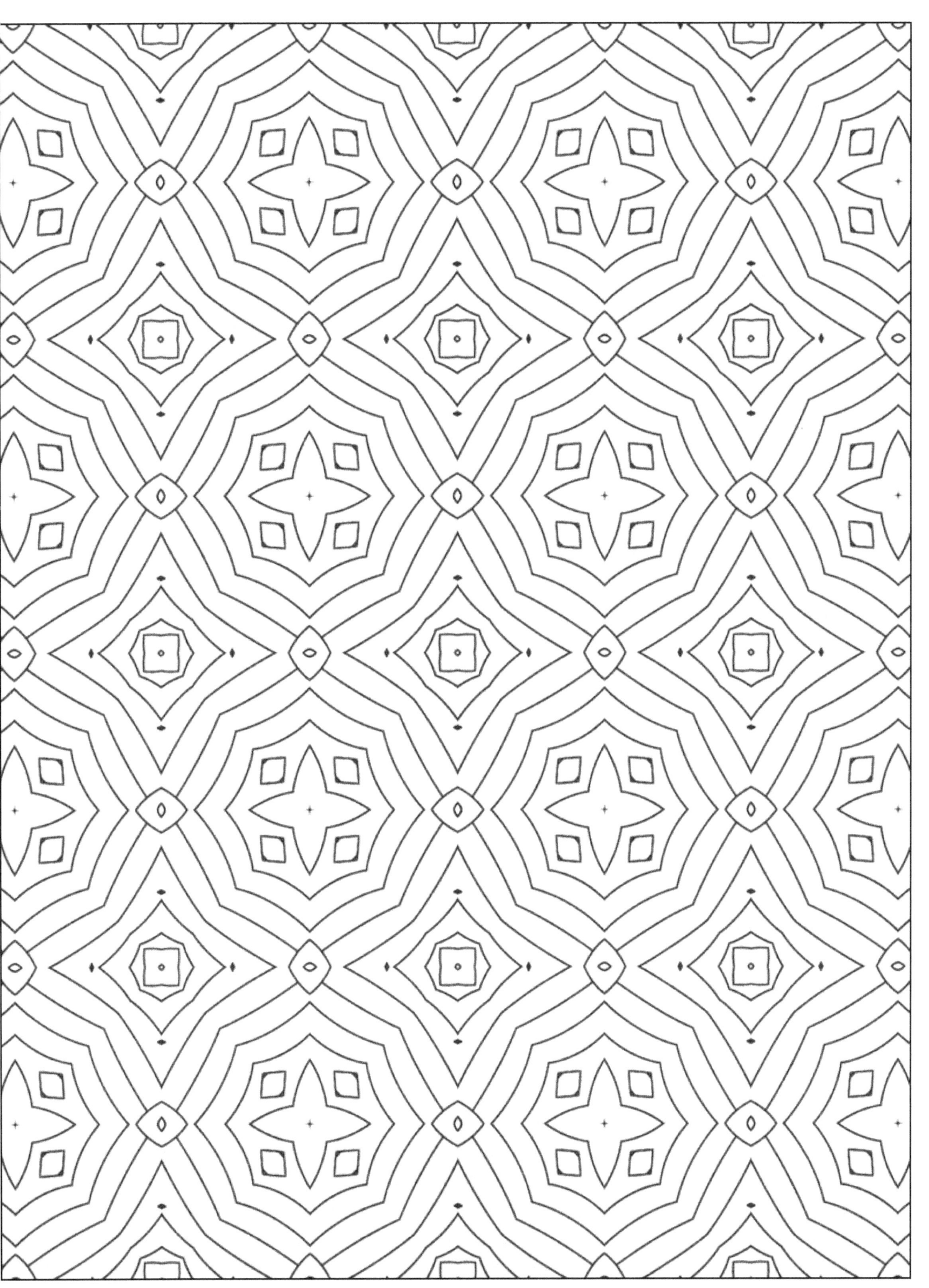

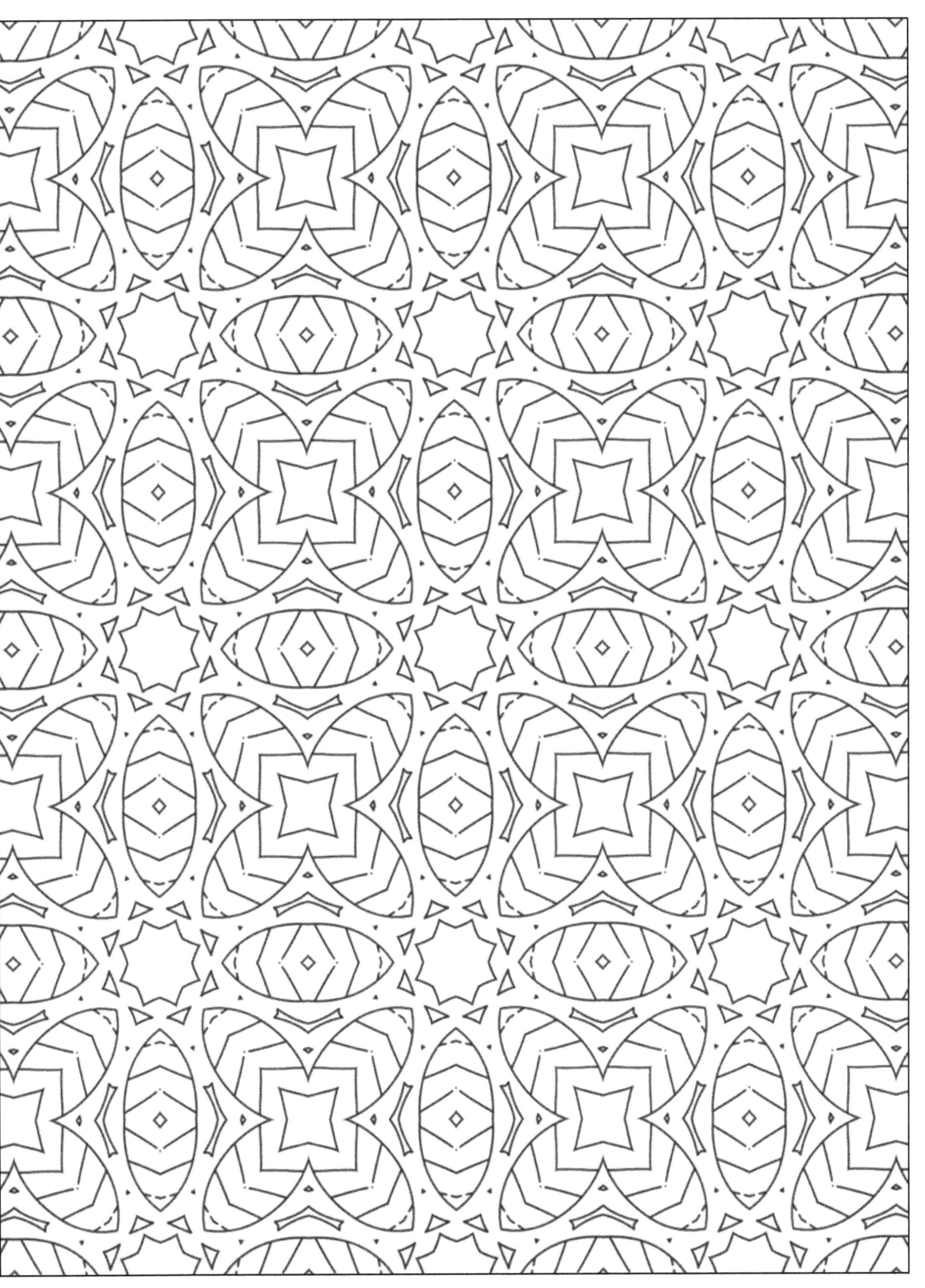

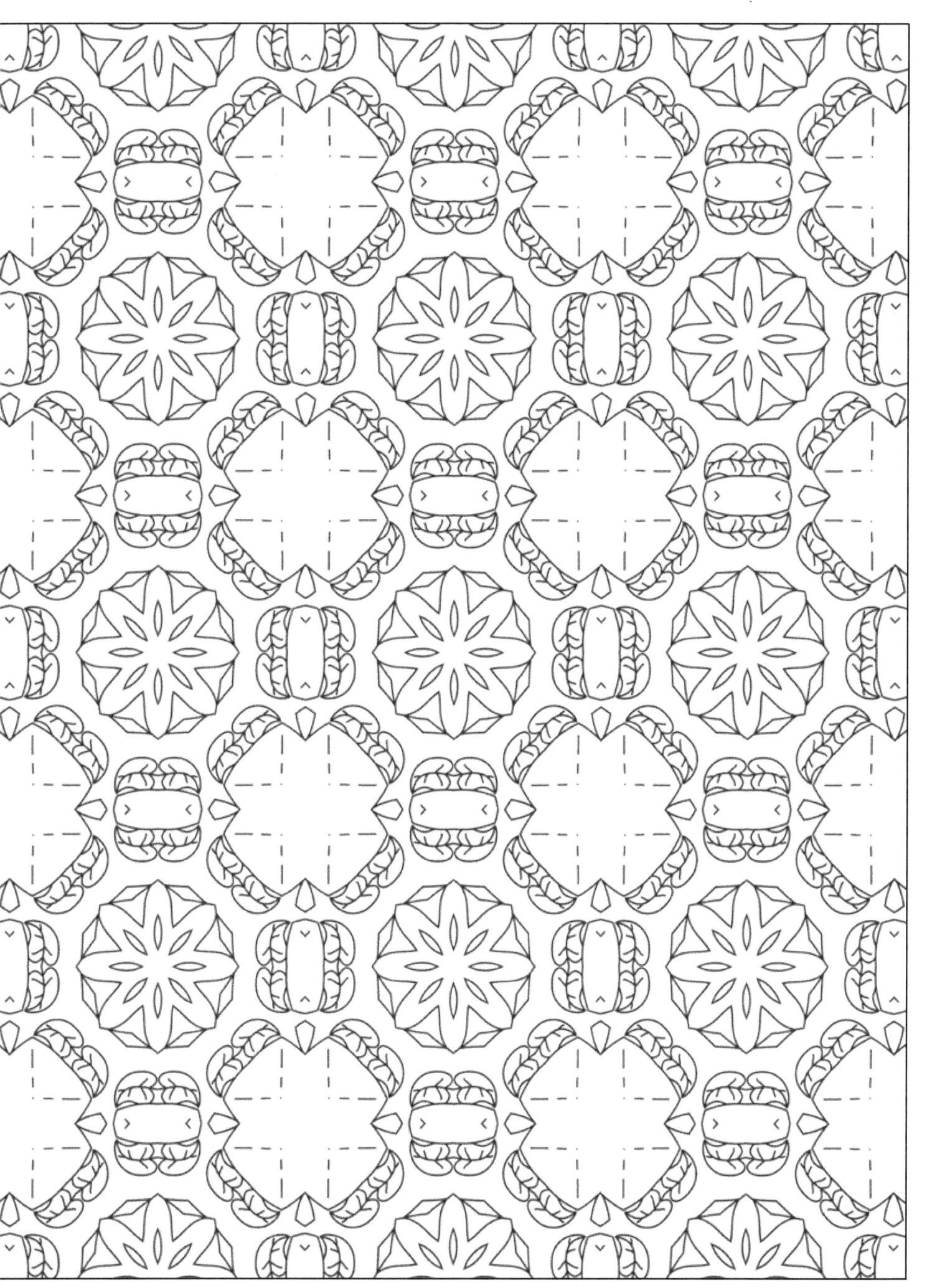

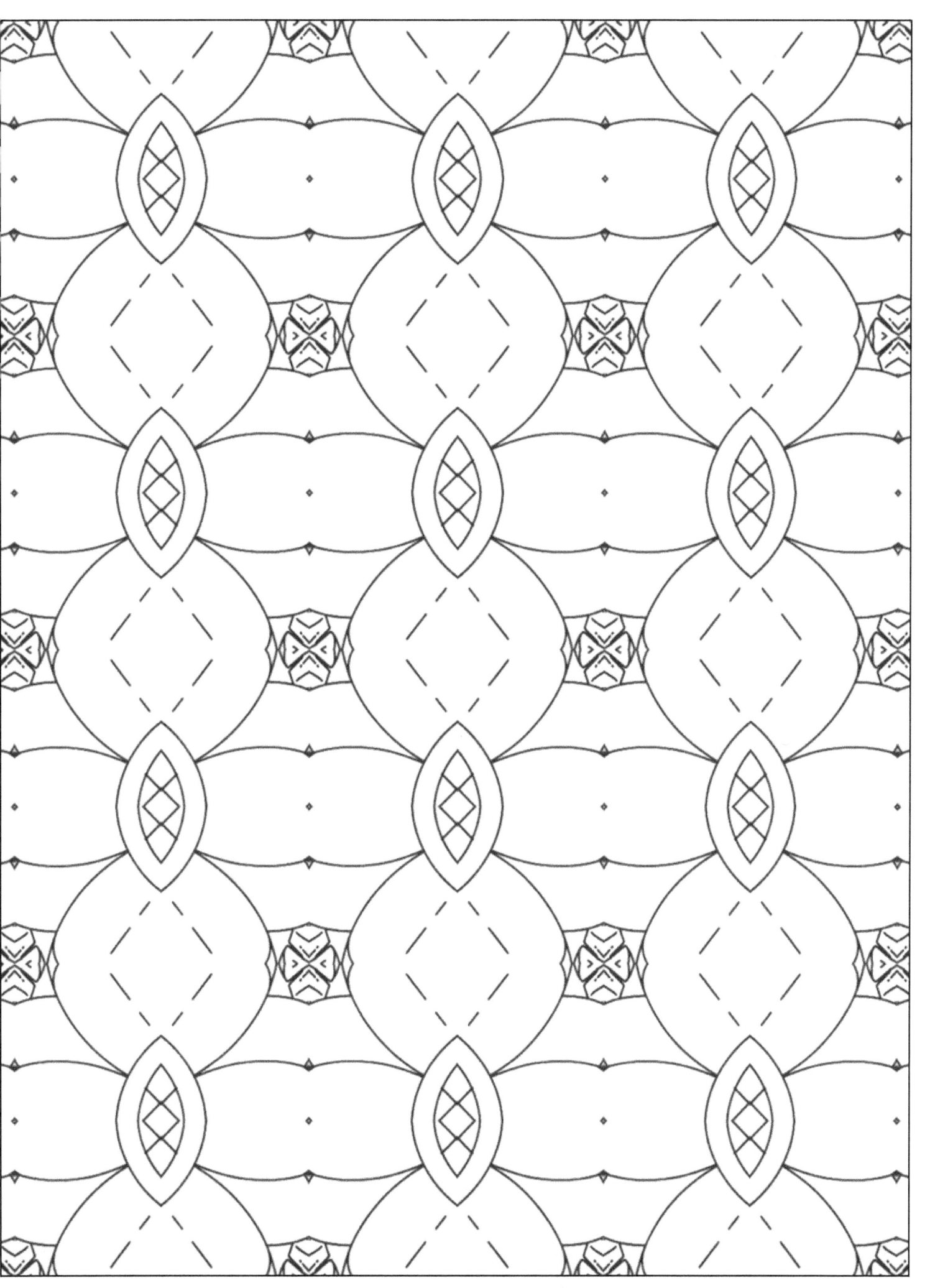

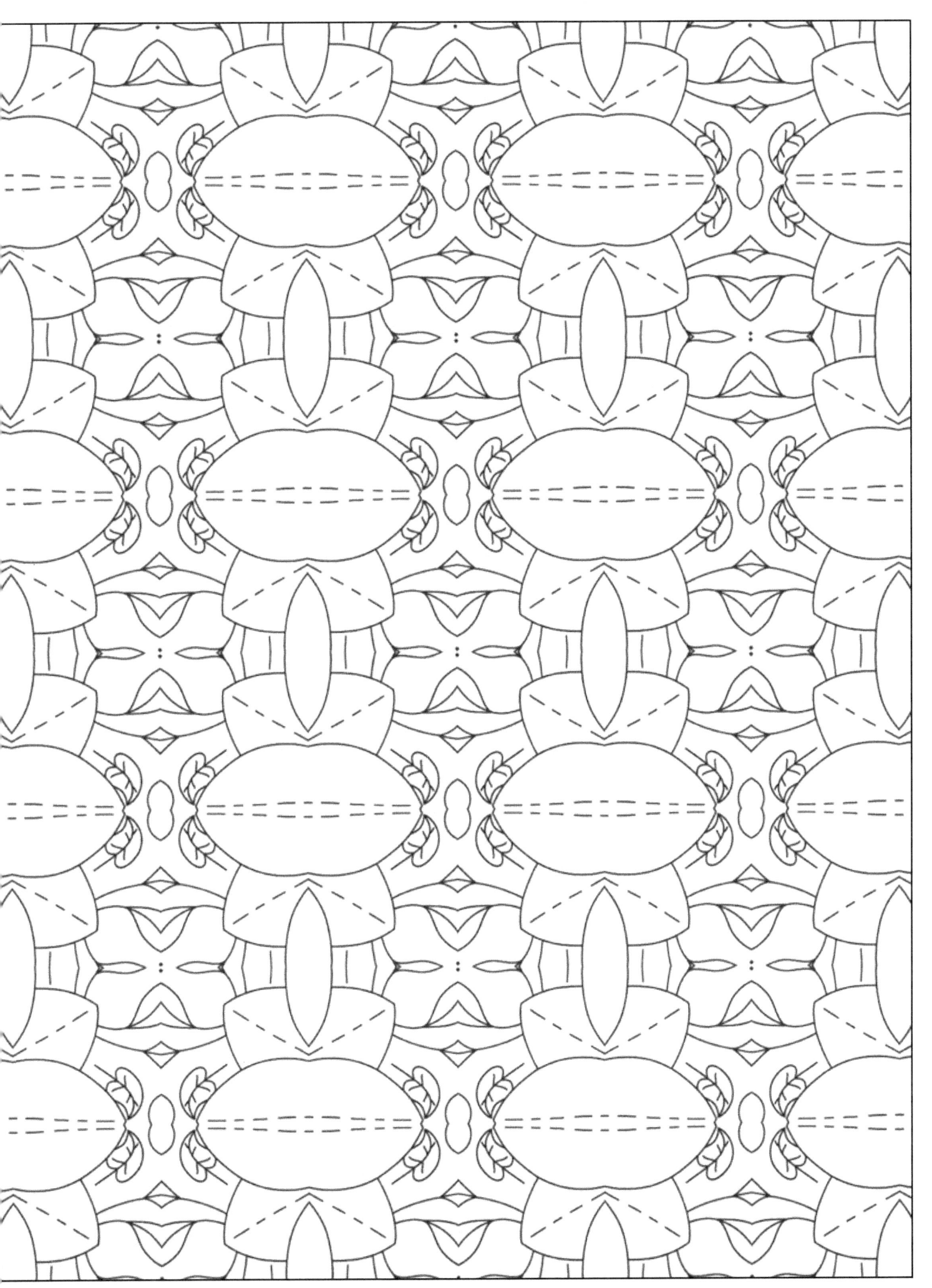

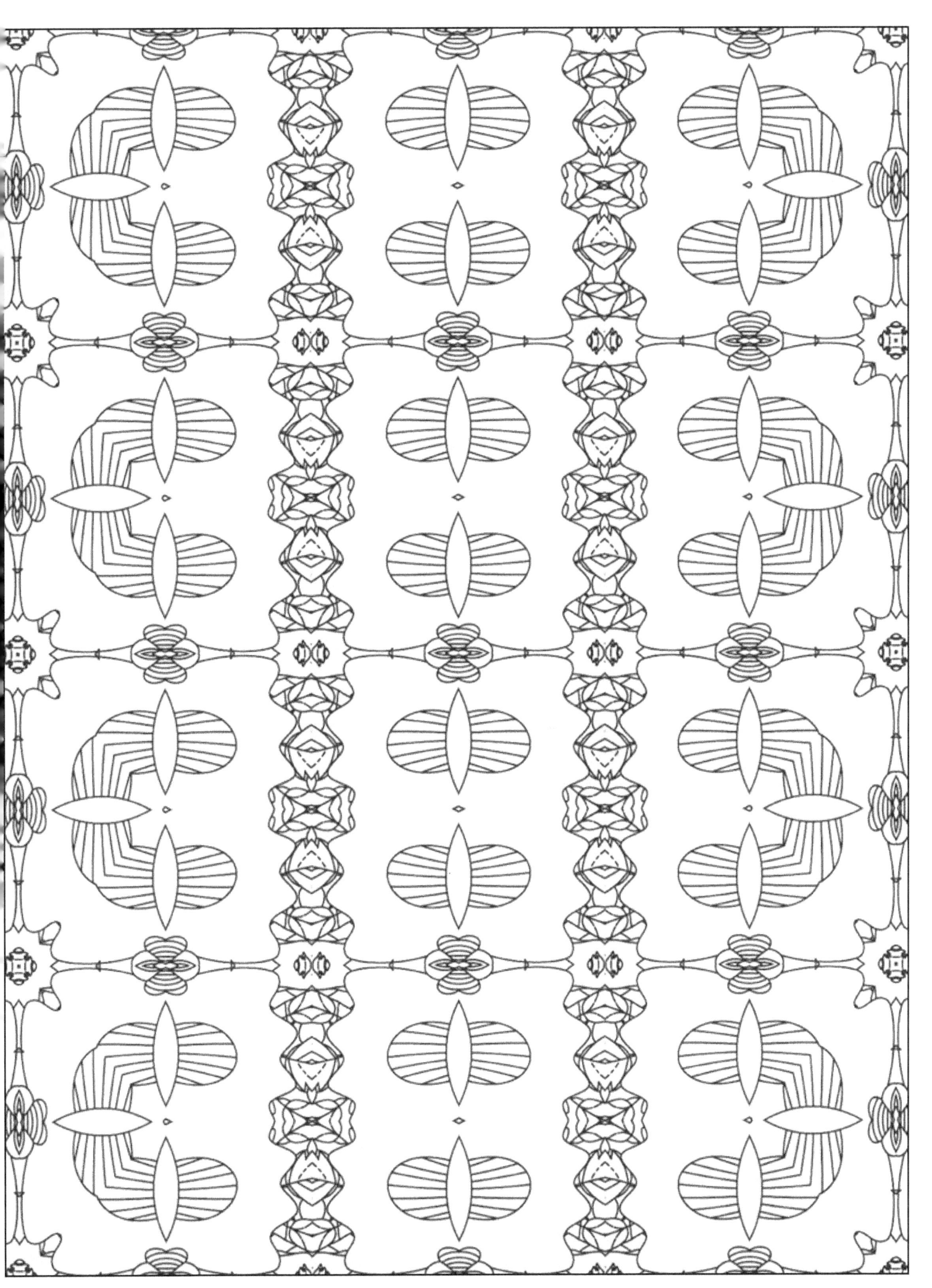

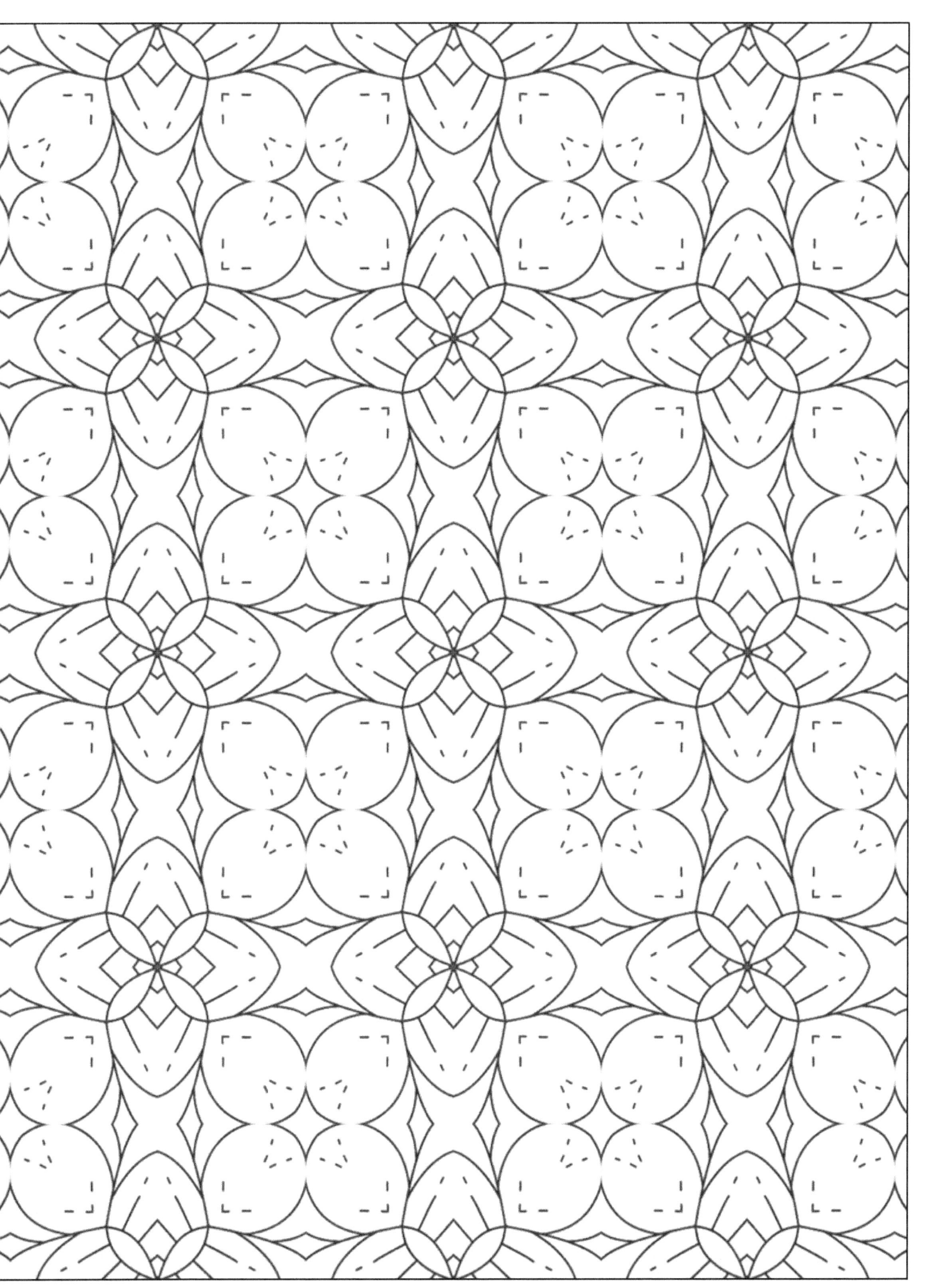

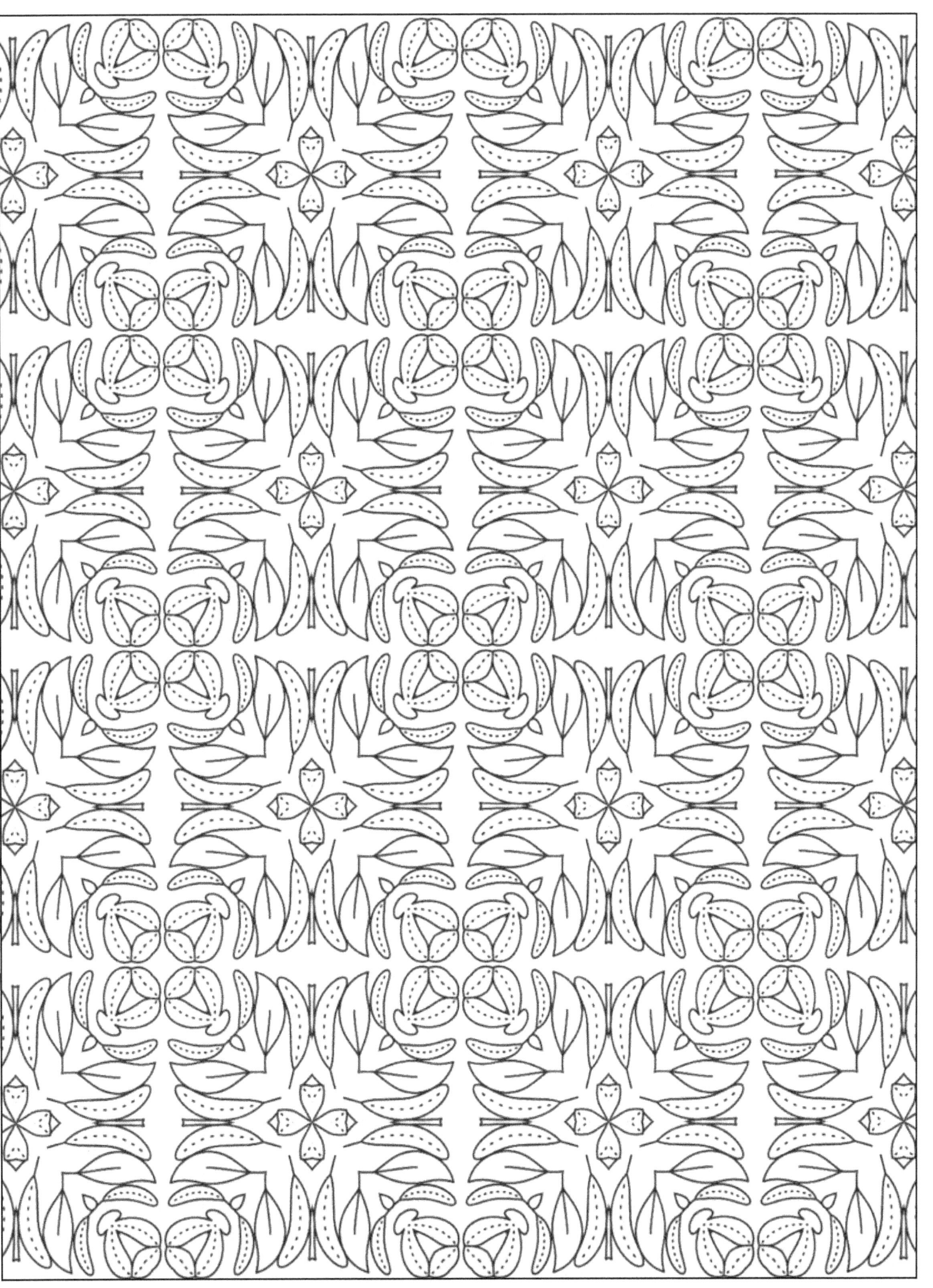

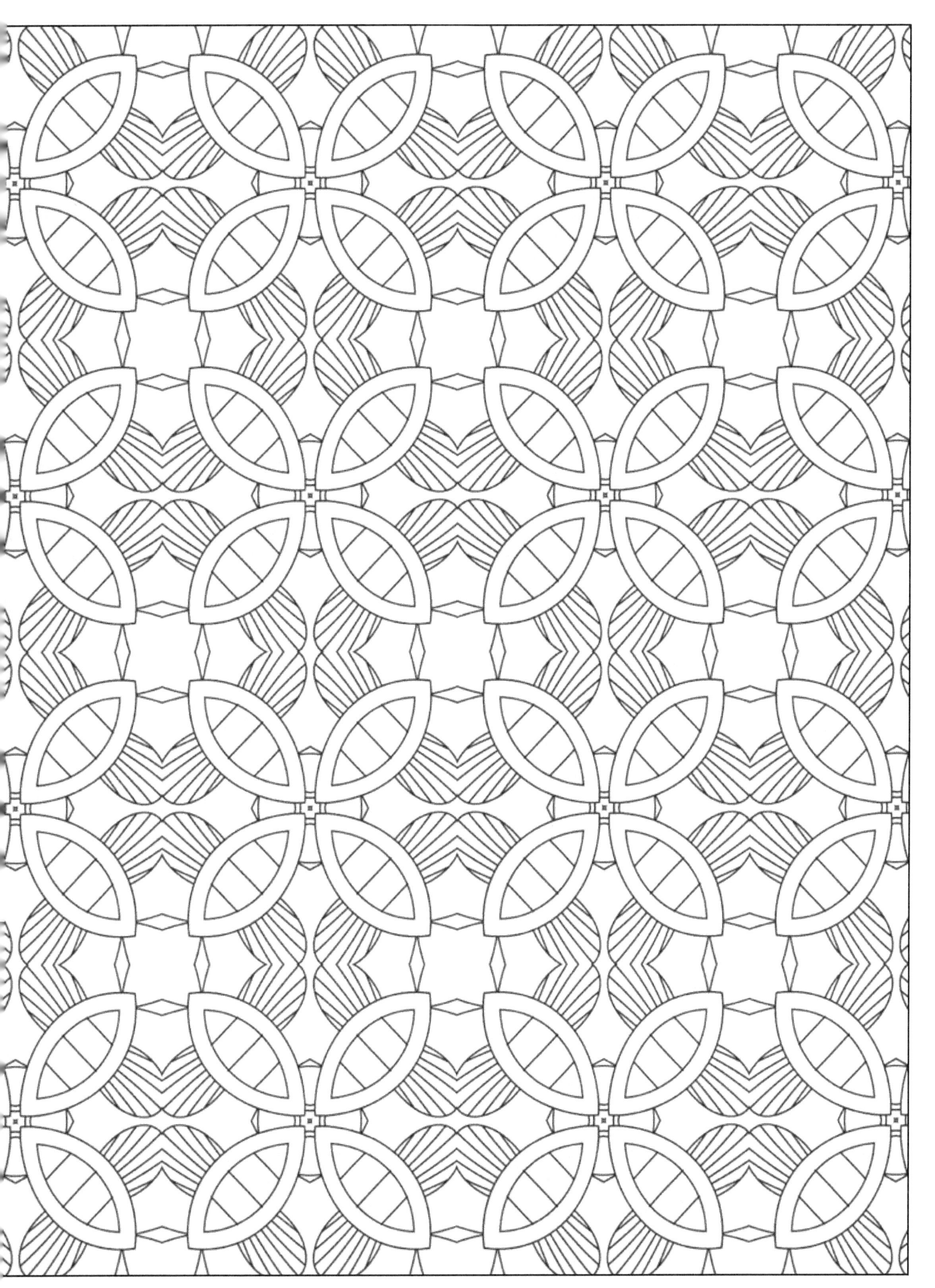

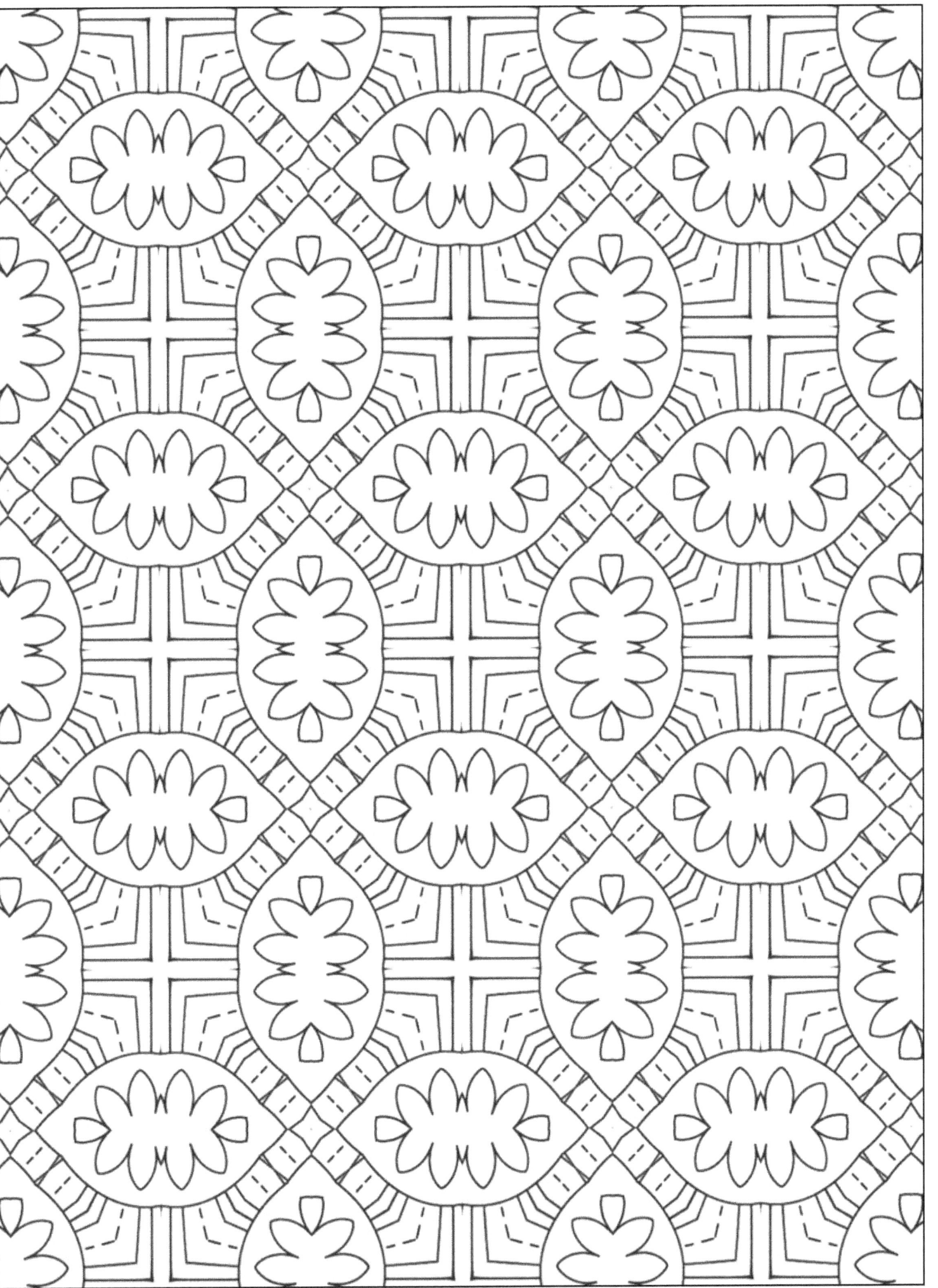

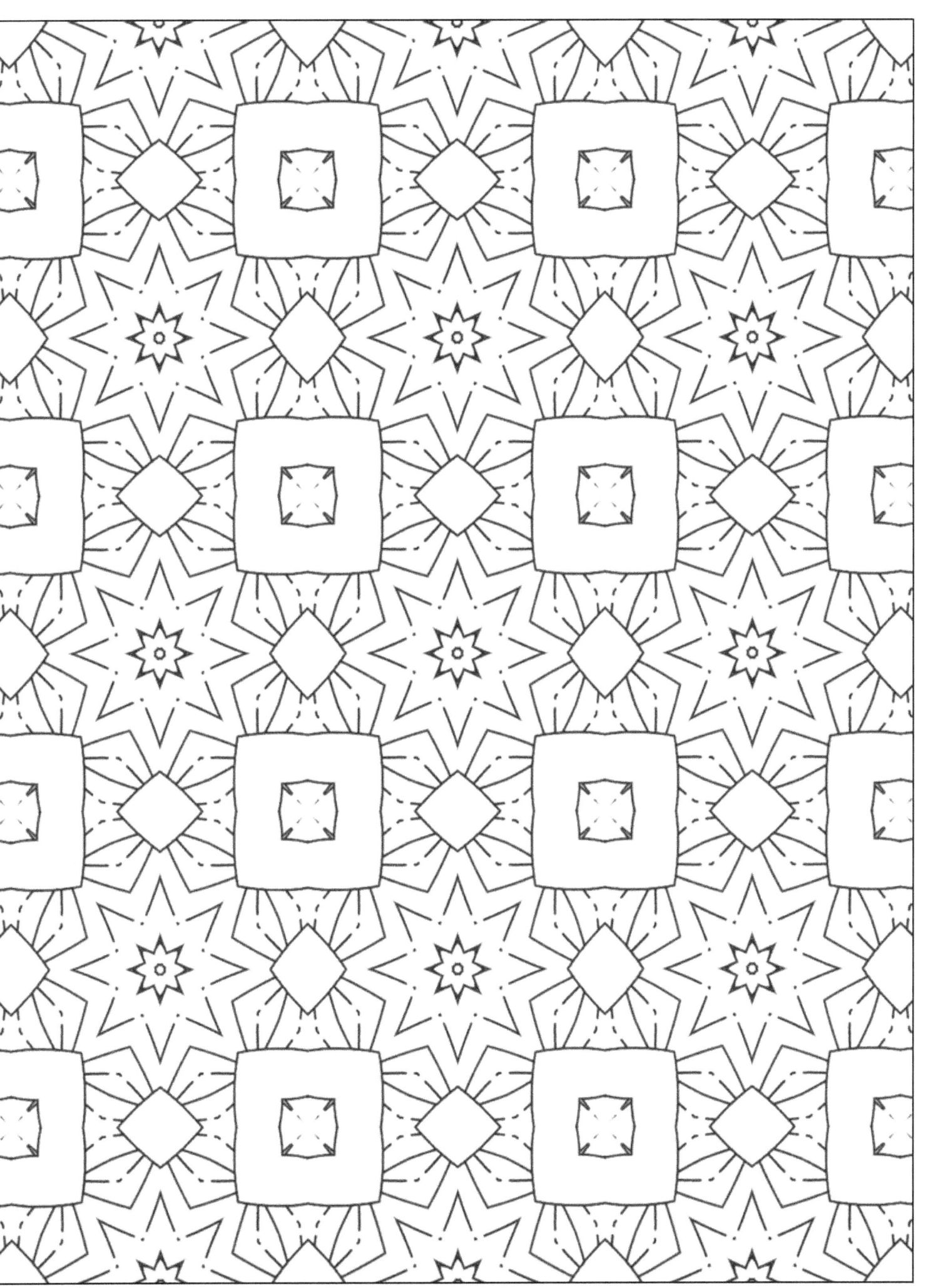

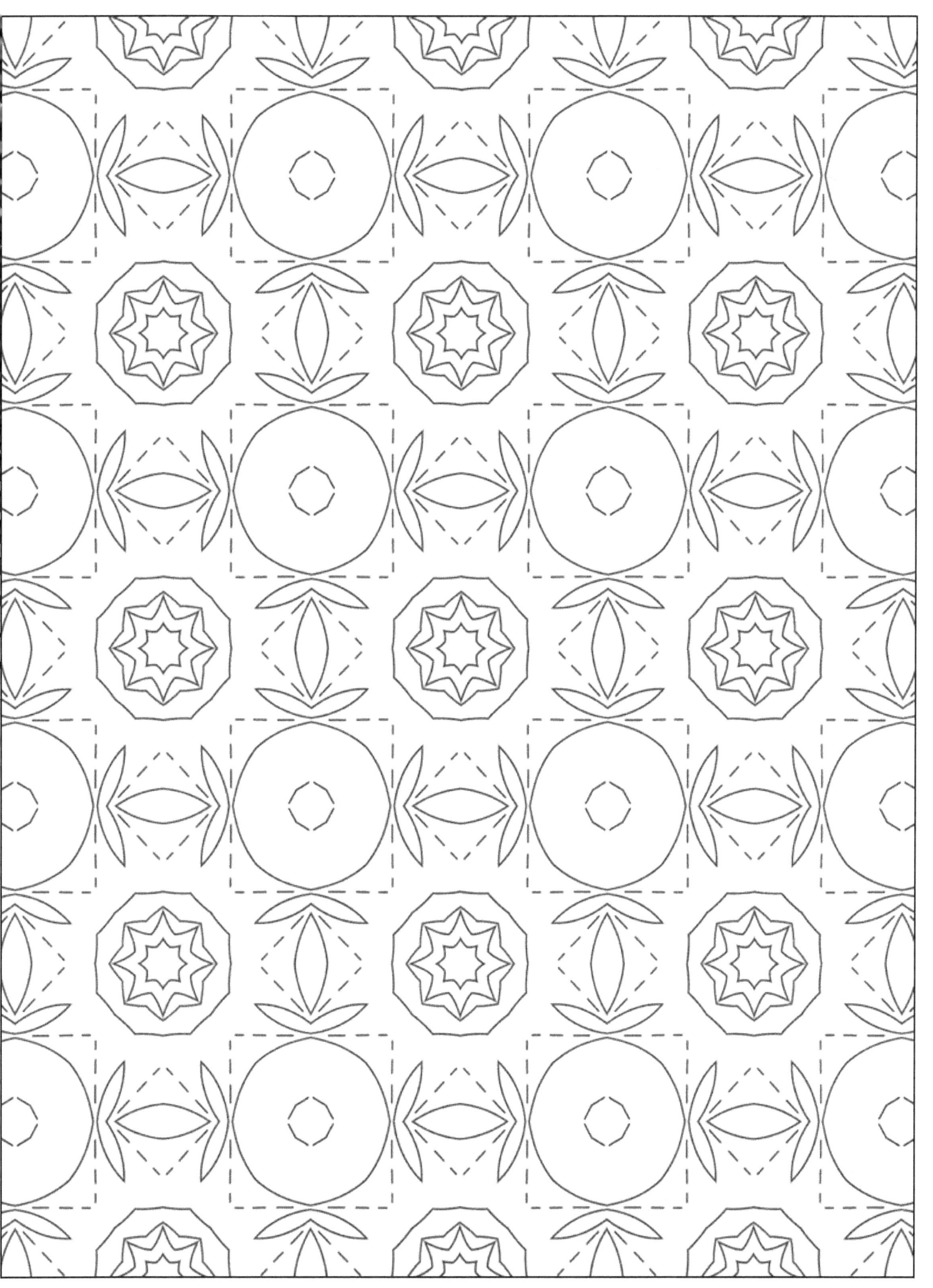

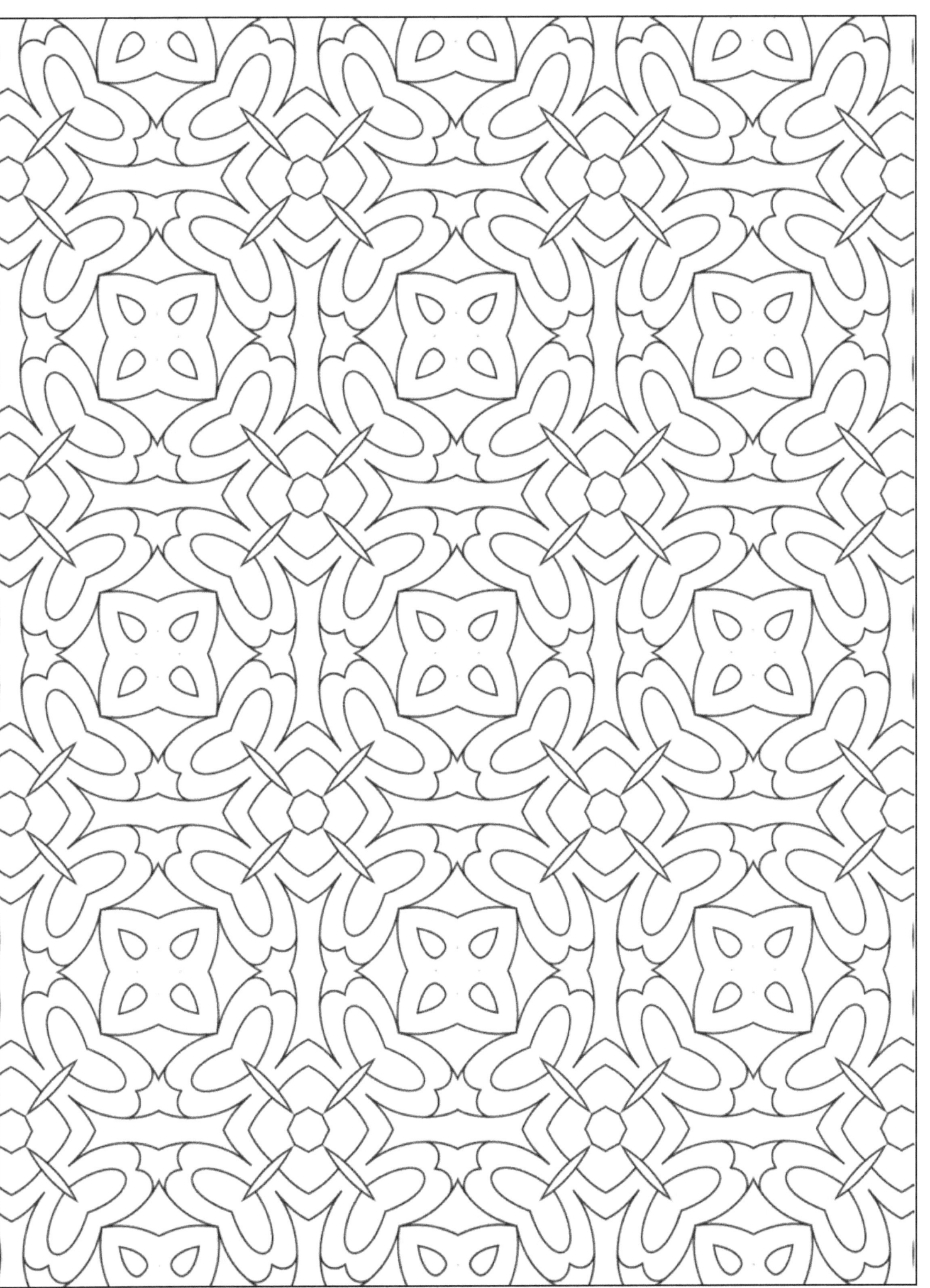

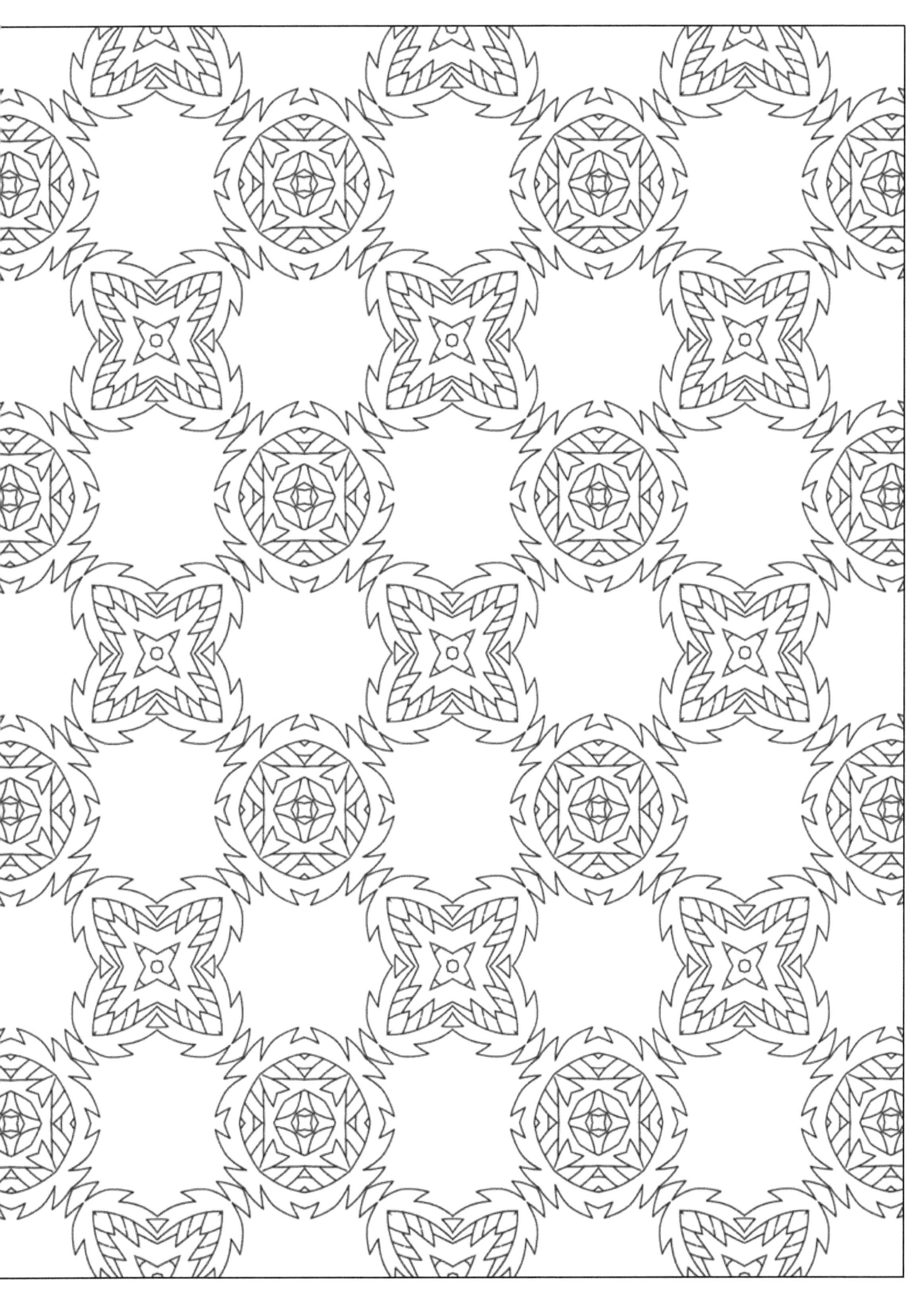

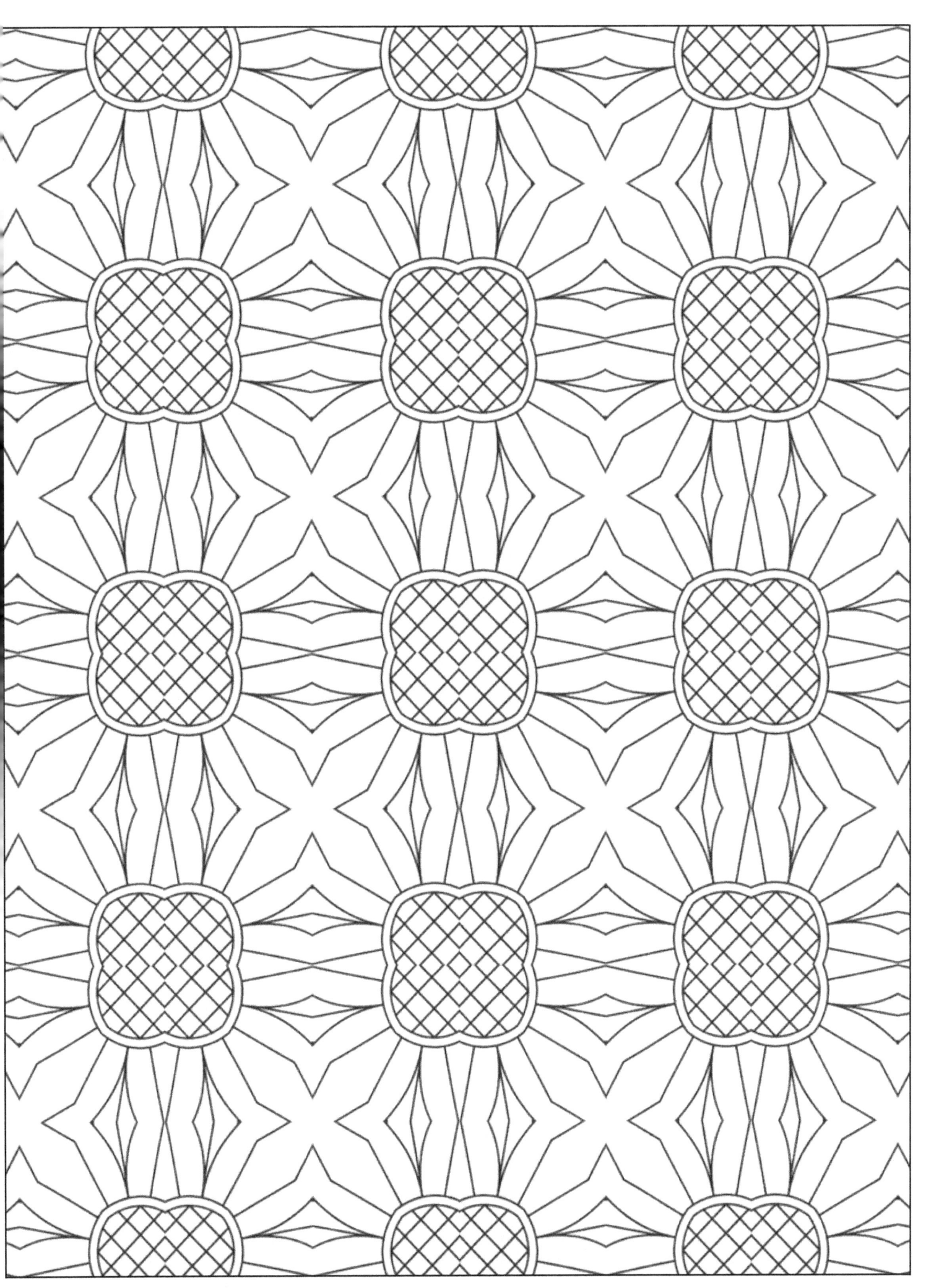

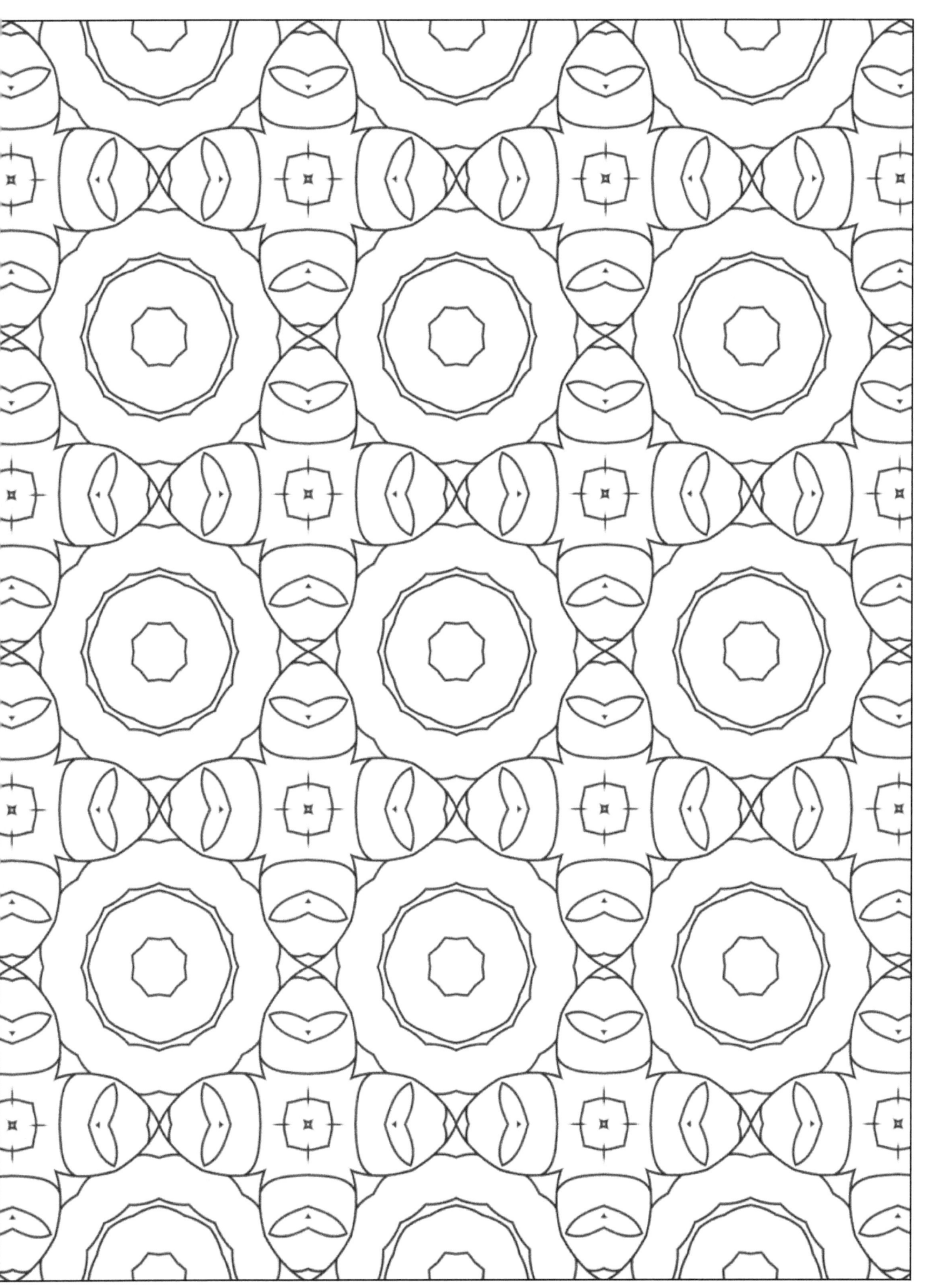

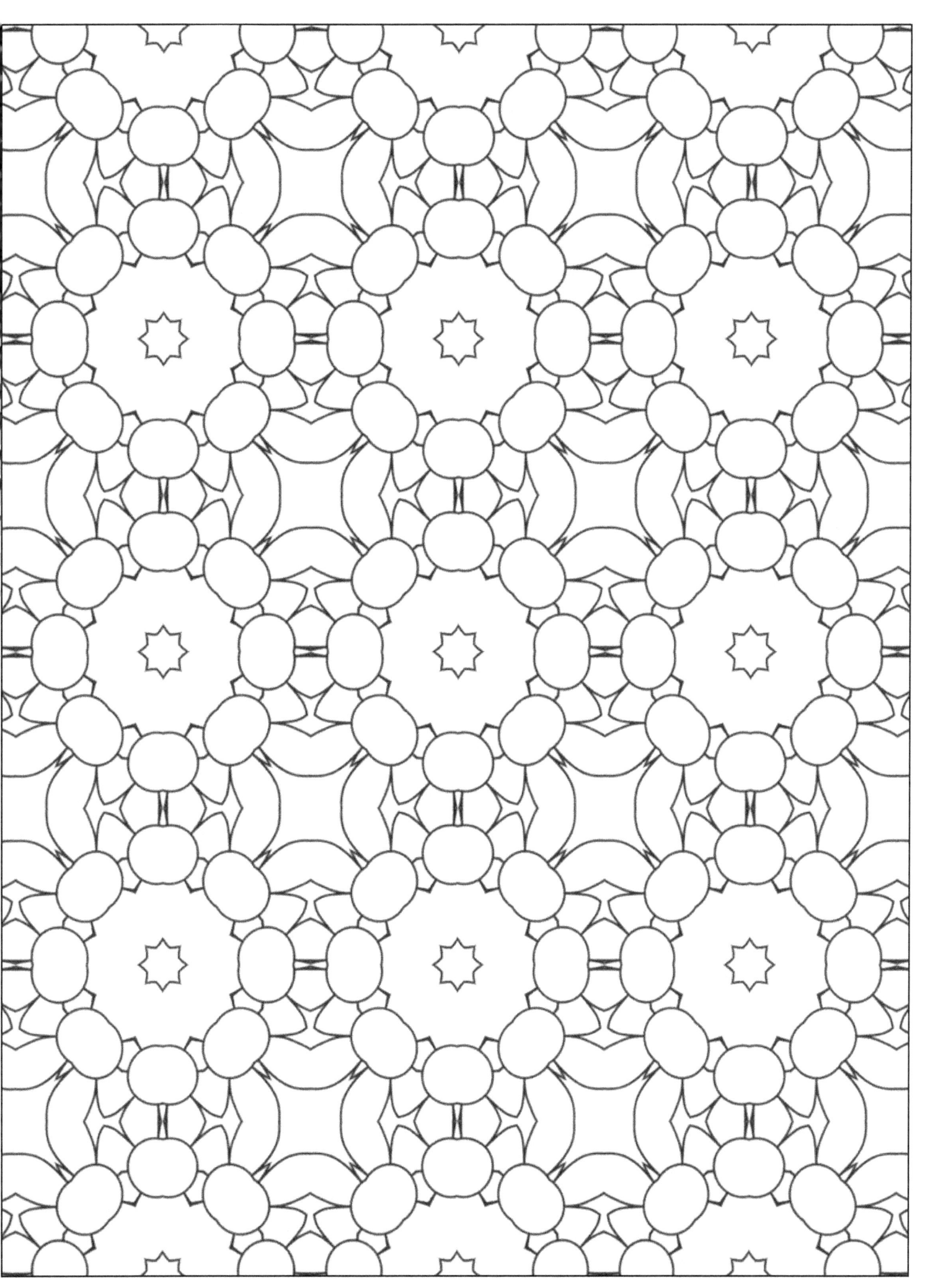

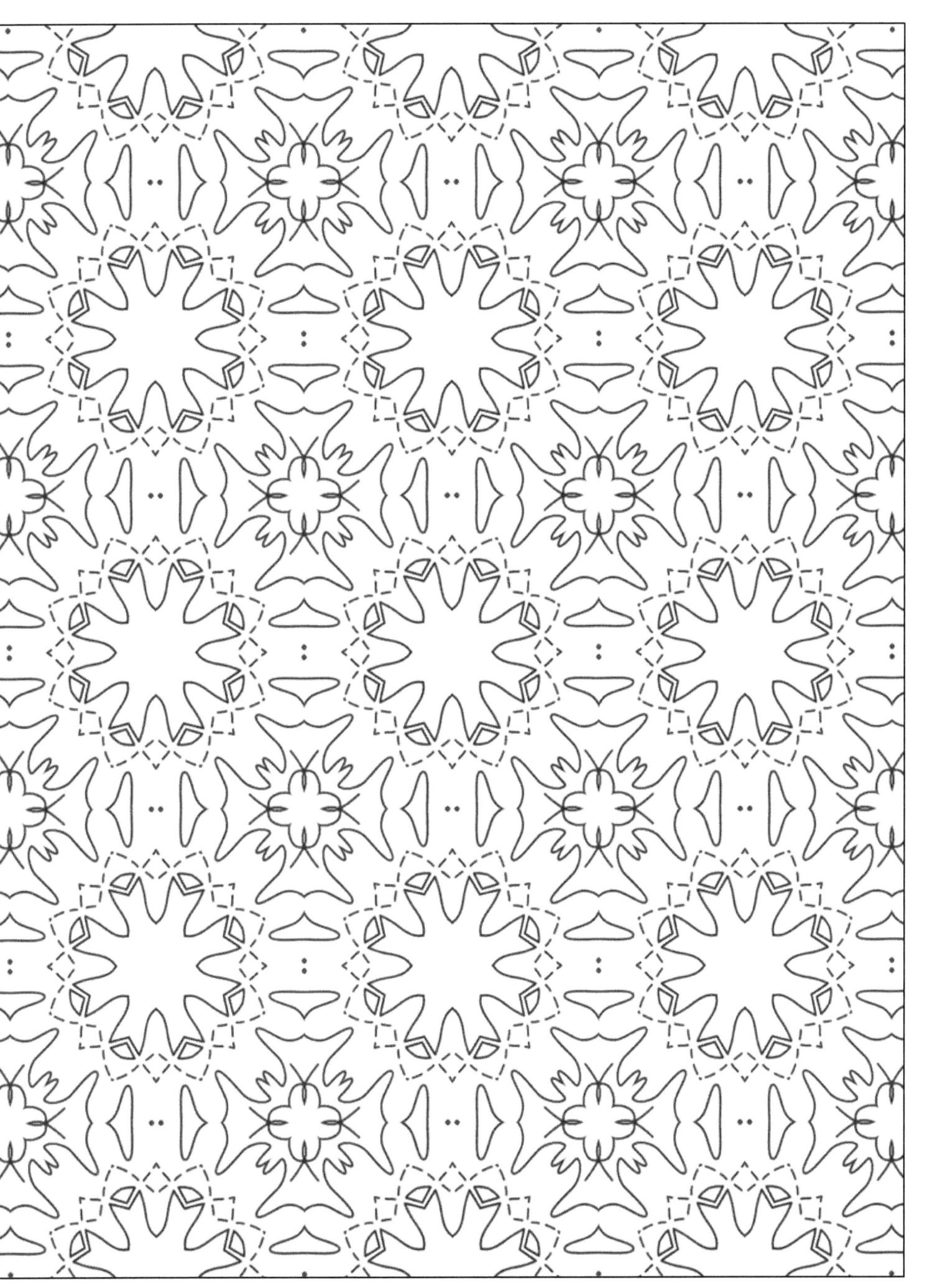

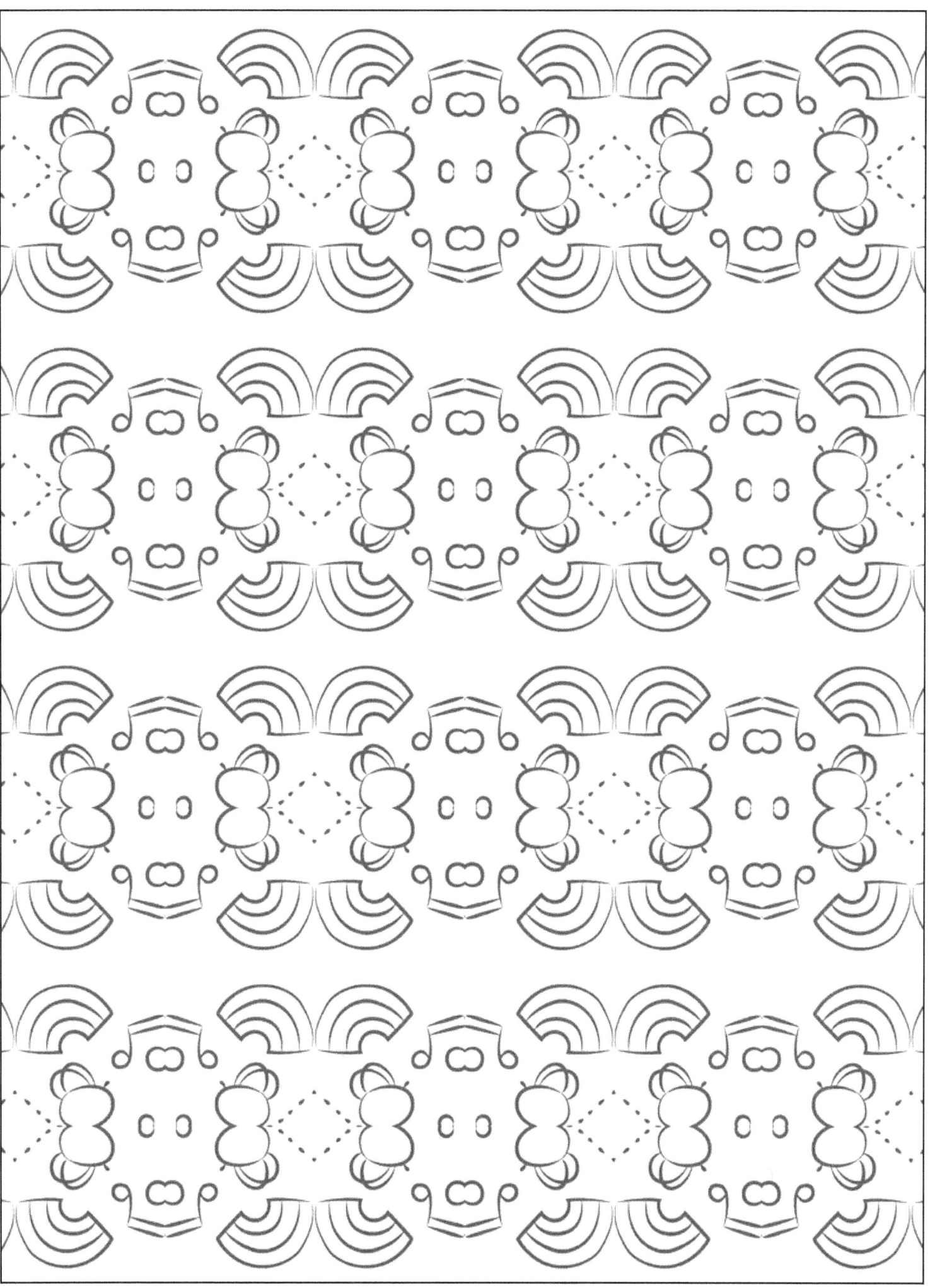

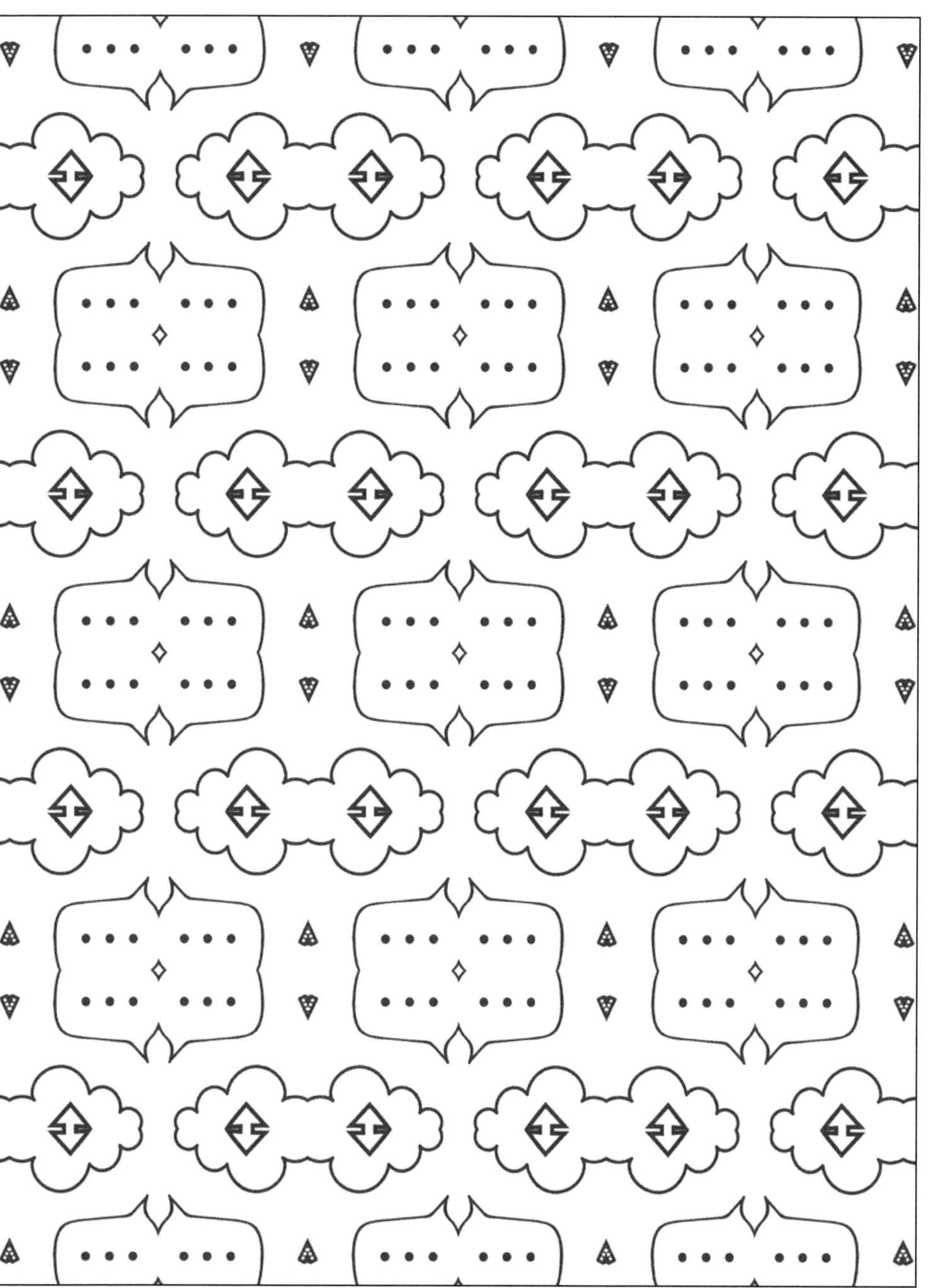

Coloring Activities Benefits

1. Creates Hand-Strength

Perhaps the most compelling motivation shading is significant at this age is on the grounds that it creates hand strength. As grown-ups, we've been writing, typing, and doing fine engine abilities for quite a long time which implies we underestimate our hand strength. Babies and preschoolers, in any case, are simply starting to construct those muscles. Hand strength is significant for all hand-related fine engine aptitudes, particularly penmanship. Composing takes strength and smoothness, and shading helps practice these muscles. Hand strength will likewise uphold your youngster's legitimate pencil hold.

2. Offers Practice for Pencil Grip

A colored pencil is likely one of the main composing instruments your kid will hold. By rehearsing with pastels, your kid is tweaking their appropriate pencil grasp. Pencil grasp is part hand strength and part practice. Shading takes into consideration both! Most ill-advised hand holds are caused when a kid creates helpless grasp propensities before their hands are sufficiently able to help the correct grasp.

3. Invigorates Creativity

Allowing a youngster the chance to shading invigorates the innovative focuses in their psyche. Tones, shapes, translations, and envisioned stories are on the whole present when a kid is shading. Regardless of whether your youngster draws a similar picture again and again, they're actually captivating the imaginative focuses in the cerebrum that cycle tones and shapes.

4. Energizes Self-Expression

Whenever youngsters have the occasion to shading, they draw in their freedom and self-articulation. What tones would it be advisable for them to pick? What would it be a good idea for them to draw?

What will it resemble? Will it be huge or little? Will it have bunches of shadings or only one tone?
Will the countenances be grinning or scowling? Odds are, the solutions to their inquiries are either intentionally or subliminally communicating or their feelings.
Drawing is an opportunity for your youngster to work through their feelings and to communicate in a protected climate. Youngsters may not generally have
the words to state precisely how their inclination, however shading will let your kid communicate without requiring the jargon to do as such.

5. Improves Fine Motor Coordination

In youth, youngsters are as yet building up the fine engine coordination abilities that will in the end uphold their day by day exercises.
Typing, writing, cooking, family tasks, turning pages of a book, utilizing devices, doing their hair — basically everything requires engine aptitudes. At the point when your kid tones, the person is building up their fine engine coordination. Other shading related exercises that help grow fine engine coordination incorporate spot to-speck pictures, following, shading inside the lines of shading pages, playing spasm tac-toe, and duplicating an image onto a clear piece of paper.

6. Creates Focus

Shading is additionally an incredible center structure work out. Center is a significant aptitude for kids to learn, for their scholastic vocations as well as for their expert professions too. Center is the thing that encourages us see through any assignment beginning to end.
You'll see as your youngster's center builds up that their drawings become more mind boggling, setting aside more effort to finish.

www.ingramcontent.com/pod-product-compliance
Lightning Source LLC
Chambersburg PA
CBHW081655220526
45466CB00009B/2768